— but you can be touched by me,

— I can take you on a journey,

ps — when your eyes are closed,

What am I?

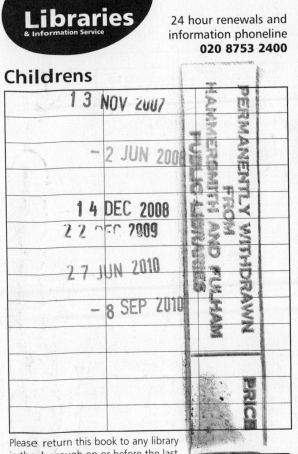

For Duncan Williamson (the Jack of Riddles,
King of Songs and the Ace of Tales) — H. L.

For Alessandro, such a kind riddle — S. F.

Barefoot Books
124 Walcot Street
Bath BA1 5BG

First published in Great Britain in 2003 by Barefoot Books, Ltd
This paperback edition printed in 2007

This book has been printed on 100% acid-free paper

Colour separation by Bright Arts, Singapore
Printed and bound in China by PrintPlus Ltd

This book was typeset in Book Antiqua
The illustrations were prepared in china ink and watercolour on 100% cotton 300gsm watercolour paper

Paperback ISBN 978-1-905236-33-6

British Cataloguing-in-Publication Data:
a catalogue record for this book is available from the British Library

1 3 5 7 9 8 6 4 2

Riddle Me This!

Riddles and Stories to Sharpen Your Wits

Retold by **Hugh Lupton**

Illustrated by **Sophie Fatus**

Barefoot Books
Celebrating Art and Story

Contents

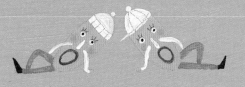

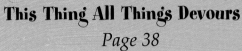

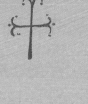

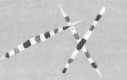

Introduction

Riddles are like tiny poems. They take an everyday thing that we've seen a thousand times and they describe it in a way that makes us see it as if for the first time. When we guess (or hear) the answer, we think, 'Of course!' The answer is funny and clever and beautiful. Take, for example, this riddle from Lapland: 'A man a hundred years old wears a hat that is only a day old. What is it?'

When we hear the riddle a thousand possible answers go rattling through our minds, but when we arrive at the right one — a tree covered with snow — there is a moment of delight, the world is made richer by a twist of language, by a simple picture in the mind's eye. And once we've got the answer we can take the riddle to someone who hasn't heard it. Now we are in a position of power. This is another of the pleasures of riddling; it's called 'being in the know'.

Ever since language began, riddles have been enjoyed. Every country in the world has hundreds of them. Why? Because we are all caught up in questions and answers. We learn to ask the question 'Why?' when we are two years old and we don't stop asking it for the rest of our lives. Life is a bundle of riddles.

Some of them we can answer, some we can't. One of my favourite authors, Alan Garner, has written: 'We tell stories to unriddle the world.' I think what he's saying is that when scientific knowledge can't find the solution to a problem, when something is too strange and mysterious to be explained rationally, then the riddle-language of story might be able to get us closer to the truth.

In this book I've brought riddles, riddle-poems and riddle-stories together from many cultures and countries. Some of them I like because they've made me laugh, others because they've surprised me into thinking about the world in new ways. I hope you enjoy them as much as I do.

Hugh Lupton

Little Nancy Etticoat

Little Nancy Etticoat in a white petticoat and a red nose,

The longer she lives the shorter she grows.

What goes up the chimney down,
But can't go down the chimney up?

What comes once in a minute,

Twice in a moment,

But never in a thousand years?

Brothers and sisters have I none,
But that man's father is my father's son.

Who is he?

What sits in the corner and travels around the world?

A House Full

A house full,
a hole full,
You cannot fill
a bowl full.

By night they come without being fetched,

By day they are lost without being stolen.

In marble halls as white as milk,
Lined with skin as soft as silk,
Within a fountain crystal clear
A golden apple does appear.
No doors there are to this stronghold
Yet thieves break in and steal the gold.

Light as a feather with nothing in it,

A strong man can't hold it

Much more than a minute.

When the horse strokes the cat
The wood begins to sing.

Two Travellers in Arkansaw

Arkansas, USA

'Halloo, farmer.'

'Halloo, strangers.'

'Can you tell us where this road goes?'

'Well, in all the years I've been here, it ain't gone any place yet.'

'Have you lived here all your life, farmer?'

'Not yet, strangers.'

'We're lost, farmer, we're tryin' to find our way home. Can you help us?'

13

'Well, if I was lost I wouldn't start here.'

'Farmer, why don't you mend the roof of your barn?'

'When it rains it's too wet for the job; when it's dry it's as good as any man's barn.'

'Farmer, I reckon you ain't too far from a fool.'

'Well, there's only a gate between us.'

'Now, let me just count on my fingers, strangers ... I reckon it adds up to one hundred exactly. One of me and two nothings of you.'

'Farmer, how deep is that ford through the creek?'

'Well, it'll barely cover the bottom half of a duck.'

'Farmer, I bet you can't even count. There's two of us

and one of you — how many is that altogether?'

'Farmer, you *are* a fool.'

'Maybe I am, but then again, I ain't lost.'

15

Two Legs, Three Legs, Four Legs

Two legs was sitting on three legs holding one leg,

Along came four legs and seized one leg,

So two legs picked up three legs and threw it at four legs,

And four legs brought back one leg.

What is it that the more you take away,

The larger it becomes?

What has six legs,
Two heads,
One tail and
Four eyes?

What is a hundred years old and wears
A hat that is only one day old?

A Bottom at the Top

What has a bottom at the top?

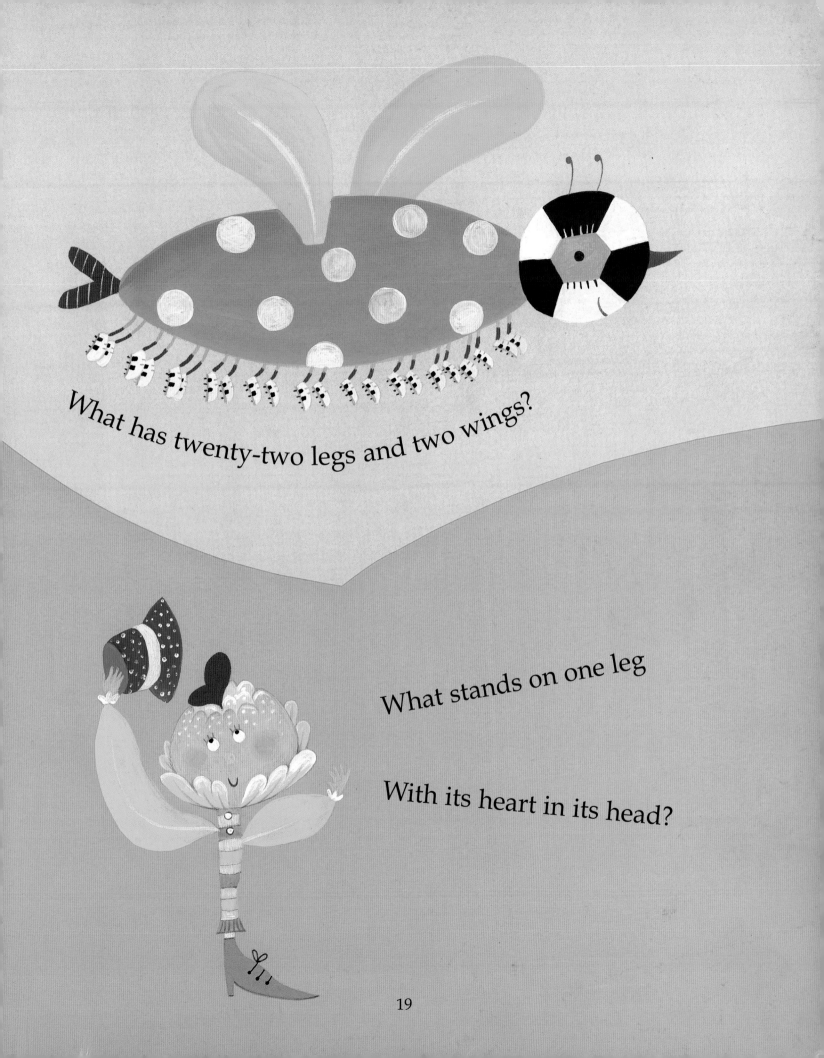

What has twenty-two legs and two wings?

What stands on one leg

With its heart in its head?

19

The Best and the Worst in All the World
Cuba

Old King Alligator was coming to the end of his days. Nobody loved him. He had been a cruel king. Now he was old and alone, his teeth were yellow, his eyes were dim and his scales were tarnished.

In the back of his mind one question troubled him: Who would follow him to the throne? Who would rule over the country when he was gone?

Years ago he had eaten all his children; just to make sure that they didn't cause him any trouble, he'd eaten every single one of them (he was an alligator after all). Now he wished he hadn't.

'Just one son,' he thought to himself. 'If only there was just one handsome son or a beautiful daughter to take my place.'

One day, as he was sitting on his throne with these thoughts turning slowly in his mind, a young alligator burst into the room. He was magnificent, his teeth white and sharp as knives, his eyes bright, every scale shining like a jewel. He bowed.

'Father!' he said.

'Father?'

'Father! I am your secret son. My mother hid me from you. I grew up far away across the world. Now I have returned. I am young and strong and clever.

Give me your golden crown. Your throne should be mine now.'

Old King Alligator looked the youngster up and down. He smiled and then he scowled. Filled with admiration and jealousy, he both liked and hated what he saw.

'I can see that you are young and strong and bold — just as I was once when I was in my prime. But are you clever?'

The young alligator smiled:

'Test me.'

The old king thought. He thought for a long time. Then he lifted his head.

'Very well, I will set you two tasks. The first is this: I want you to make me a meal out of the best thing in all the world.'

The young alligator bowed and left the throne room. He began to search. He searched lakes and lagoons, mountain tops and sea beds. He searched forests and deserts, cities and farms. He visited the finest markets and the poorest kitchens. Suddenly he knew what to do. He found what he was looking for. He cooked it slowly and carefully with spices and herbs. He poured an exquisite creamy sauce over it. He brought it to Old King Alligator steaming on a silver platter.

'Here is a meal made of the best thing in all the world.'

The old king tasted it.

'Mmmm, delicious, delicious … what is it?'

The young alligator smiled.

'Between heaven and earth there flies a red bird that is always wet. You tell me what it is.'

22

The old king ate and thought, he thought and ate, and every mouthful tasted better than the one before.

'I don't know, tell me more.'

'A soft innocent that always lies between two assassins. Now tell me what it is.'

The old king finished the meal and licked his lips with his long, red, wet …

'Aha! I have it. It is a tongue!'

The young alligator nodded:

'It is a tongue — that can lull a baby to sleep, that can fill the ears and the heart with love and delight, that can make peace between two warring armies and can lead the world into truth. Truly it is the best thing of all.'

The old king sighed:

'You are right, and I wish mine had done such things. But now for your second task: I want you to make me a meal out of the worst thing in all the world.'

The young alligator bowed and left the throne room. He began to search. He searched lakes and lagoons, mountain tops and sea beds. He searched forests and deserts, cities and farms. He visited the finest markets and the poorest kitchens. Suddenly he knew what to do. He found what he was looking for. He dipped it into a pool of slimy water. He pushed a stick into it and held it over a smoking fire. He sprinkled it with ashes and he brought it to Old King Alligator on a wooden board.

'Here's a meal made of the worst thing in the world.'

The old king lifted it to his mouth and tasted it. He spat it out.

'Pta! Disgusting, disgusting … what is it?'

23

The young alligator smiled.

'It is the whip that can lash itself as well as others. You tell *me* what it is.'

The old king ate and thought, he thought and ate, and every mouthful tasted worse than the one before.

'I don't know, tell me more.'

'There are thirty-two white stools ranged around the long red room where this old gossip lives.'

The old king dipped his mouth into a tub of water, trying to wash the taste from his long, red, wet …

'Aha! I have it. It is a tongue! But how can the best thing also be the worst?'

The young alligator replied:

'A tongue can fill a child with fear, it can fill minds and hearts with hatred, it can bring two countries to the brink of war and it can lead a whole people into slavery.'

The old king sighed.

'You are right, and many times has mine done such things. A tongue is truly the best thing and the worst thing in all this world … and now my throne and my golden crown are yours.'

And Old King Alligator hobbled away and was never seen again.

A Great Wonder

On the way I saw a great wonder:

Water had turned to bone.

The Thief of Words

A moth devoured words.

When I heard of that wonder it seemed strange —

That a thief should swallow a song,

That a thief should eat a great man's speech.

And for all his labour, that thief was no wiser —

For the words he had swallowed.

Something was here since the world first began
Yet is never more than a month old.

Something dead sits on something alive,
That sits on something dead,
That sits on something alive,
That stands on something dead,
That sits on something alive.
What is it?

What is put on a table, cut, but never eaten?

The Snake of Dreams
Georgia, Russia

Once upon a time — and it was neither my time nor your time — there lived a great king.

And one night that king dreamed a strange dream.

He dreamed that a fox was hanging by its tail from the ceiling above his golden throne, a red fox, snarling and snapping, suspended by its red brush.

When the king woke up, he called for all his advisers and all his wise men.

'What could be the meaning of such a dream?' he asked.

But they all shook their heads and shrugged their shoulders and not one of them could find an answer to that question. So the king ordered every grown man and woman in his kingdom to gather before the palace.

'Surely,' he thought to himself, 'there must be someone in this great country who can unriddle my dream.'

So the people came from north, south, east and west. And among the many there was one, a simple farmer, who lived among the mountains far in the north. As he travelled towards the king's palace, he came to a narrow pass between two mighty mountains, and curled in the dust of the road there was a snake. As the farmer drew close, the snake lifted its thin head:

'Aaaaaah, traveller, stop, and tell me where you are going.'

The farmer stopped in amazement.

'I … I … I'm going to the palace — the king has had a dream.'

'And traveller, do you know the meaning of this dream?'

'Me, I'm just a farmer; I know nothing about dreams.'

'Well, traveller, I can tell you its meaning, and if you tell the king he will reward you well.'

'Then tell me, snake, tell me now!'

'Aaaaaah, traveller, nothing comes from nothing. I will tell you only if you promise to share half of that reward with me.'

'I promise, snake; now tell me.'

'The king has dreamed of a fox, hanging above his throne, and the dream means thisssss —'

The farmer crouched down and the snake lifted its thin head and whispered into his ear.

The farmer listened, nodded and continued his journey, and after some days he joined the massing crowd before the king's palace. A trumpet sounded, the king's dream was told, and a great hush fell on the people. No one could unriddle the dream.

But then, from the back of the crowd, came a voice:

'Majesty, majesty, your dream means this —'

'Bring the man forward!'

And the farmer was brought before the king.

'Majesty, your dream means this: These are times of cunning and treachery, no one is to be trusted, your kingdom is like a den of foxes.'

The king nodded and smiled.

'The dream is well read.'

From beneath his throne he took two bags of gold and gave them to the farmer.

And the farmer set off for home, but he was careful to avoid the pass between the mountains; he went the longer way round and kept all the gold for himself.

And time passed.

Then one night the king dreamed a second dream.

He dreamed that a sword was hanging by a hair from the ceiling above his golden throne — a sharpened sword, flashing and spinning, suspended by a fine thread.

And when he woke he called his messengers:

'Go and fetch that farmer from the north!'

When the farmer received the king's message, his heart sank, but he knew there was only one thing for it, and he set off along the narrow pass between the two mountains.

'Snake, snake!'

There was no answer.

'Snake, snake, I need your help again!'

'Aaaaaah, traveller, I am here.'

'The king has had a second dream.'

'I know, and I will tell you its meaning, but only if you truly promise to share half of your reward with me.'

'This time, snake, I truly promise.'

'The king has dreamed of a sword, hanging above his throne, and the dream means thisssss —'

And the snake whispered into the farmer's ear.

The farmer continued his journey, and after some days he was standing before the king's throne.

'Majesty, your dream means this: These are times of anger and warfare, your enemies are preparing for battle, your kingdom is bristling with sharpened swords.'

The king nodded and smiled.

'The dream is well read.'

He gave the farmer four bags of gold, and he prepared himself for battle.

As for the farmer, this time he followed the narrow pass between the mountains, but when he saw the snake curled in the dust of the road waiting for him he was filled with anger and he drew his knife.

'Aaaaaah, traveller,' said the snake, 'you have brought me my share!'

'You'll have nothing but a black stone and a cinder!'

He chased the snake and hacked off its tail with his knife.

And he kept all the gold for himself.

And time passed.

Then one night the king dreamed a third dream.

He dreamed that the carcass of a sheep was hanging by its legs from the ceiling above his golden throne — a fat, dressed carcass, skinned and split like meat in a butcher's shop.

When the king woke he sent his messengers to fetch the farmer again.

And the farmer knew there was only one thing for it. Swallowing his pride, he set out for the third time along the narrow pass between the mountains.

'Snake, snake!'

There was no answer.

'Snake, please, snake, forgive me!'

There was no answer.

'Snake, I need you again.'

'Aaaaaah, traveller, I am here.'

'Snake, I beg you to forgive me; the king has dreamed again.'

'I know, and I will tell you the meaning, if this time you swear to share your reward with me.'

'I swear, half will be yours.'

'The king has dreamed of a sheep's carcass, hanging above his throne, and the dream means thisssss —'

The farmer listened and continued his journey. Soon enough he was standing before the king's throne.

'Majesty, your dream means this: These are times of ease and generosity,

33

every belly in the land is full, your kingdom is like a fat carcass giving peace and plenty to all.'

The king nodded and smiled.

'The dream is well read.'

He gave the farmer six bags of gold, and the farmer made his way straight back to the pass between the mountains.

'Snake, snake!'

The snake came and the farmer knelt beside it with tears in his eyes.

'Snake, now you must take all these six bags of gold, for truly it is half of all that I have won — and I have no words to tell you my shame at having treated you so badly.'

But the snake lifted its thin head and shook it sadly from side to side.

'Traveller, traveller, you have done no wrong, there is no blame. You are just one among many. When the kingdom was like a den of foxes, you too were treacherous and cunning and you went home the other way and kept all of the gold. When the kingdom was bristling with sharpened swords, you too were quick to anger and you cut off my tail. And now that the kingdom is like a fat carcass giving peace and plenty to all, you too are suddenly filled with kindness and you offer me your gold. But, traveller, what use have I, the oldest of the old and the wisest of the wise, for your paltry gold? Keep it and go in peace.'

With that the snake slid into a crack in the rock and was gone.

And the farmer swung the bags over his shoulders and continued his journey — but suddenly the gold seemed heavy against his back.

Two Brothers

Two brothers we are,

Great burdens we bear,

By which we are bitterly pressed;

The truth is to say

We are full all the day

And empty when we go to rest.

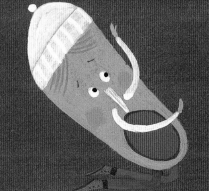

You go into it through one hole,

You come out of it through three holes,

When you're inside it you're ready
to go outside,

When you're outside you're still inside.

What is it?

What belongs to you but others use it more than you do?

Placed above, it makes things smaller.

Placed beside, it makes things greater.

In matters that count, it always comes first.

Where others increase, it remains the same.

What is it?

Those that have eyes have no head,
Those that have heads have no eyes.

What gets wetter the more it dries?

This Thing All Things Devours

Gollum's Riddle

This thing all things devours:
Birds, beasts, trees, flowers;

Gnaws iron, bites steel;

Grinds hard stones to meal;

Slays king, ruins town,

And beats high mountain down.

The Riddle that Killed Homer

All that we caught we threw away,

All that we didn't catch we kept.

The Sphinx's Riddle

What is it that goes on four legs

in the morning,

on two legs at noon, and on three in the evening?

The Mad Hatter's Riddle

Why is a raven like a writing desk?

King John and the Bishop of Canterbury

England

Once upon a time there lived a king. His name was John and he was a bad and a greedy king.

Now King John had a bishop, the Bishop of Canterbury, who was widely loved for his kindliness and his saintliness.

The more John heard of the bishop, the more he hated him. One day he sent his armed henchmen to Canterbury to fetch him. The humble bishop, dressed in a monk's hood and habit, was bound in iron chains and dragged before the king.

King John looked him up and down.

'I hear that you are loved by the people.'

The bishop bowed his head.

'Maybe this is true, your majesty.'

'I hear that they love you more than they love me — their king and monarch.'

The bishop said nothing.

'And so I am minded to cut your shaved head from its shoulders, but I am a merciful man, so I will spare your life —'

'Thank you, your majesty.'

'I will spare your life, if you can answer me three little questions.'

The king chuckled and the bishop bowed his head again.

'I will do so, my lord, as far as my poor wit can extend.'

'The questions are these. First: How much am I worth? Second: Where is the centre of all the world? Third: What am I thinking?'

The bishop shuddered.

'Your majesty is jesting …'

'You will find it no jest if you cannot find the answers. You have one little week before your head bids farewell to its shoulders. Begone!'

Well, the poor bishop left King John's palace in fear and trembling. He made his way to Oxford and put the questions to some of the most learned scholars in the land — but not one of them could help him. Finally he made his way home to Canterbury to say his farewells to the people who loved him.

As he was drawing close to the city, he met an old shepherd on the downs. The old man waved his crook in the air.

'Welcome home, Lord Bishop. What news from London?'

'Sad news, bad news, my friend.'

And the bishop told him all that had taken place.

'Not such bad news, my Lord Bishop, for maybe an old fool could answer what a wise man cannot. Let me go to London in your place. Let me wear your hood and habit, swap your crozier for my crook, and if I lose my head the world will be none the worse for it.'

'Thank you, thank you, old man,' said the bishop. 'But I must face this danger myself. You and I are hardly twins, the king will quickly know he is being fooled and then we will both lose our heads.'

But the shepherd would not listen.

'With a hood drawn down over my face, he will not be able to tell us apart.'

In the end the bishop was persuaded. The shepherd made his way to the king's palace with his head bowed, his hood drawn down, and a silver crozier in his hand.

'Aha,' said King John, 'you have come, Lord Bishop, and are ready to meet your doom!'

'I am ready for your questions, your majesty.'

'We'll start with the first. How much am I worth?'

'Twenty-nine pieces of silver.'

The king's forehead darkened into a frown.

'The King of England is worth only twenty-nine silver pennies. Why?'

'Well, your majesty, Jesus Christ was sold for thirty pieces of silver, and surely even you are not worth quite as much as Him.'

King John laughed.

'Well answered, my Lord Bishop. Now for the second question: Where is the centre of all the world?'

'Here,' said the shepherd, tapping his crozier against the ground, 'right here; and if you don't believe me, go and measure it for yourself.'

'Aha, a shrewd and a merry answer. There's more to you, my Lord Bishop, than I had thought. Now for question number three: What am I thinking?'

'That is easy, your majesty. You are thinking that I am the Bishop of Canterbury, but as you can see —' and he pulled the hood back from his face '— I am only a poor shepherd, come on bended knee to beg for his life and mine.'

The shepherd dropped to his knees before the king's throne.

King John threw back his head and roared with laughter.

'Your quick wits have saved you both — you should be bishop and he should be shepherd!'

'Only for a day, your majesty; I can neither read nor write.'

'But you can spend, I have no doubt.'

The king dropped a purse of golden coins into the old shepherd's hand.

'Take this reward for your answers, and tell your bishop that he has my royal pardon.'

So the shepherd made his way home to Canterbury, swapped his silver crozier for a wooden crook, and lived happily on the gold for the rest of his days.

Little Airy Creatures

We are little airy creatures

All of diff'rent voice and features,

One of us in glass is set,

One of us you'll find in jet,

T'other you may see in tin

And the fourth a box within,

If you should the fifth pursue

It can never fly from you.

Jonathan Swift

45

Two Little Windows

Two little windows
in one big house;
Many look in, but
only one looks out.

With one I am uncomfortable,
I am just right for two
And I am too large for three.
What am I?

What is it that you will break,

Even when you name it?

The more you pull its tail, the further away from you it goes.

The more you take from it in front,
The more you add to it behind.

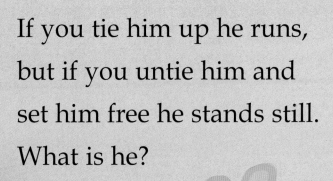

If you tie him up he runs,
but if you untie him and
set him free he stands still.
What is he?

Thin Miss Twitchett has only one eye
And a tooth that can bite you and cause you to cry,
But despite all her struggling her tail's in a trap,
Now summon your wits and riddle me that.

The Pool of Dharma
India

Once upon a time there lived five brothers — Yudhistira, Arjuna, Bima, and the golden-eyed twins Nakula and Sahadeva. They all shared the same mother, but each of them was the son of a different god and each wanted to discover the true identity of his own father.

This is the story of how Yudhistira discovered his father.

One day the five brothers were hunting in a deep forest. They were following a deer that was leaping and bounding ahead of them, flashing golden-brown in the dappled sunlight. The twins were leading the way, the other three following.

Suddenly the trees opened on to a clearing and a pool of water that reflected the clear blue light of the sky.

As soon as Nakula and Sahadeva set eyes on it, they were struck by an unbearable thirst. Their throats felt as dry as parchment. They dropped to their knees and cupped their hands in the water.

At that moment a voice came from the pool.

'Stop. Do not drink. First you must answer my questions.'

But their thirst was so acute that they could not stop. They scooped the water into their mouths and instantly fell dead beside the pool.

Then Arjuna came running into the clearing. He saw the twins lying at the edge of the water.

'My brothers!' he cried.

He sent a thousand arrows flashing among the trees — but the forest was silent and empty. Then he, too, was struck by the terrible thirst. It was as though every cell in his body ached for water.

'Stop. Do not drink. First you must answer my questions,' came the voice from the pool.

But the thirst was like a fire in Arjuna's throat; he cupped his hands, drank and fell down dead.

Great Bima burst through the trees with his club under his arm.

'Arjuna! Nakula! Sahadeva! Who has done this to you?'

He swung his club around his head, splintering trees and pounding the earth until the whole world quaked with his grief and fury. But then the thirst came, he hurled himself to the ground and plunged his face in the water.

'Stop. Do not drink. First you must answer my questions,' came the voice.

But Bima was gulping the water and soon he, too, was lying dead beside the others.

Then Yudhistira came to the clearing. He ran to the water's edge and lifted the heads of his brothers.

'I do not understand. I can see no trace of bruises or blows … and a brutal thirst grabs me by the throat.'

'Stop. Do not drink. First you must answer my questions.'

Yudhistira looked about himself — the clearing was empty, the voice seemed to be coming from the water itself.

'Who are you? I see no one. Are you in the air or the water? Are you fish, flesh or fowl?'

'It is for me to ask the questions, and for you to answer them.'

And Yudhistira, even though the thirst raged in his body like fire, forced himself to submit.

'Very well, examine me.'

'What is swifter than the wind?'

Yudhistira thought for a moment, then answered:

'The mind is swifter than the wind.'

'What does not wriggle or move after it has been born?'

'An egg does not move.'

'What forever travels alone?'

'The sun.'

'What is reborn after it has been born?'

'The moon.'

'Which came first, day or night?'

'Day, but it was only a day ahead.'

'Which animal is the slyest and most cunning?'

'The one that man has not yet discovered.'

'What are more numerous than the blades of grass?'

'Our thoughts.'

'What can cover the earth?'

'Darkness.'

'What is it that keeps a thing from discovering itself?'

'That too is darkness.'

'What makes you wealthy if it is thrown away?'

'Greed.'

'What is greed?'

'It is poison.'

'What is honesty?'

'It is to see every living creature as though it were yourself, bearing your own longing for life and your own fear of death.'

'What is the cause of the world?'

'Love.'

'Who are more numerous, the living or the dead?'

'The living, for the dead are no longer.'

'What is the rarest thing?'

'To know when to stop.'

'What is your opposite?'

'Myself.'

'What, for each one of us, is inevitable?'

'Happiness.'

'What is the greatest wonder?'

'That we live each day surrounded by death, and yet we live each day as though we were immortal.'

Suddenly, from the depths of the pool of water there came laughter — deep, booming laughter.

'My son, you have answered well and I am proud of you.'

Yudhistira looked about himself, his raging thirst had suddenly vanished.

'Who are you? Where are you?'

'I am everywhere! I am your father, Dharma. I am the pattern and order of the world, the law that underlies all creation. Because your brothers would not obey my command, I turned the pool to poison. But now that you have answered me I will give them back their lives. Pour water on to their faces.'

Yudhistira tore off his shirt. He plunged it into the water and wrung the water over the heads of his four brothers. Immediately they sat up, rubbing their eyes. They looked at one another.

'We must have been sleeping.'

Yudhistira smiled.

'Nakula, Sahadeva, Arjuna, Bima, my dear brothers, you have been more than sleeping!'

53

Open and Closed

No one sees me when his eyes are open,

But he sees me when his eyes are closed.

Through me, he who does not speak — speaks,

Through me, he who does not run — runs.

I am untruthful though I tell all truth.

Little chases big out of the room,

What is it?

A lot of little brothers
live in one house;
If you scratch their heads

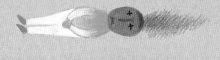

they will die.

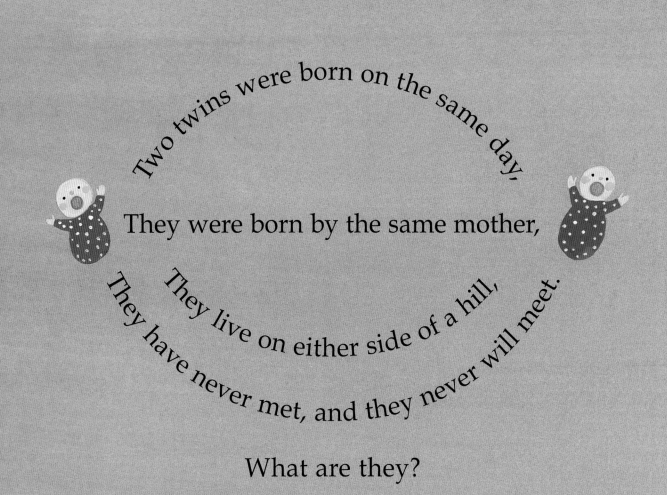

Two twins were born on the same day,

They were born by the same mother,

They live on either side of a hill,

They have never met, and they never will meet.

What are they?

Young and Old

If you had found me in my youth,

Then you would have happily drunk
the blood I shed.

But now that time has made me old,
you eat me anyway,

Wrinkled as I am, with no moisture in me,

Crushing my body between your teeth.

Where can water be found,
Coming neither from heaven
nor from the ground,
It sometimes seems sweet
and sometimes bitter,
Though it always pours forth from
the same spring?

As soon as they enter the house

They stick their heads out of the windows.

What are they?

The End of the World

Sioux

There is one riddle everyone would like to know the answer to and it is this:

'When will the world come to an end?'

Inside that cave an old woman sits, her face as shrivelled and wrinkled and brown as a walnut.

She's dressed in rawhide — the way people used to dress long ago, before the white people came.

She's been there for many thousands of years.

Beside her sits her dog. He's black with yellow eyes. He's watching her. He's watching her very carefully. He's always been there.

Here is the answer.
There is a hidden cave.
No one knows
where it is.

People have searched
for it with cars and
helicopters, with
telescopes and searchlights.
It has never been found.

She's making a blanket
strip out of porcupine
quills, flattening them
with her teeth and
threading them
together.

She's flattened so many
porcupine quills her
teeth are worn down to
little stumps. When the
strip is finished, it will
decorate her robe.

Close to where she sits there's a fire.
She lit it many thousands of years ago
and has kept it burning ever since.

Over the fire a big clay pot is hanging.
Inside the pot sweet red wojapi is boiling,
sweet berry soup. Mmmm, it smells good!

Every now and then the old woman gets to her feet and stirs the wojapi in the

clay pot. She's old and stiff and slow. It takes her a long time to stand,

As soon as her back is turned, the black dog starts pulling the porcupine quills out of

the blanket strip. He tugs them out with his teeth.

That's how it's been for thousands of years.

But one day that old woman will finish her work. One day she'll thread the last porcupine quill into the

it takes her a long time to hobble across to the fire. Her hands are

shaking. It takes her a long time to stir the soup.

When the old woman sits down, she finds her work has been spoiled.

She has to start all over again.

blanket strip and complete the pattern. One day her robe will be beautiful.

That will be the day the world comes to an end.

Notes and Sources

Stories

Two Travellers in Arkansaw

Every culture seems to have a variant on this conversation between two travellers and a not-so-foolish fool of a local. I've added elements from several of my favourites from other places to this famous Arkansas version. A fuller account of the conversation can be found in James Tidwell's *Treasury of American Folk Humor* (Crown Publishers, New York, 1956).

The Best and the Worst in All the World

I'd come across a simple version of this story from West Africa, but then I heard this wonderful Cuban variant with its riddles told by the great French/Haitian storyteller Mimi Barthélemy. It worked its way straight into my own repertoire.

The Snake of Dreams

I found this Georgian story (one of my all-time favourites) in *Folk Tales of All Nations* (Harrap, London, 1931).

King John and the Bishop of Canterbury

This story was originally a traditional ballad, 'King John and the Bishop', which can be found in volume one of F. J. Child's *English and Scottish Ballads* (Dover Publications, New York, 1965).

The Pool of Dharma

I've drawn on several versions of the great Indian epic the Mahabharata for this story, most notably *Mahabharata*, retold by William Buck (University of California Press, Berkeley, 1973), and *The Mahabharata* by Jean-Claude Carrière and Peter Brook (Methuen, London, 1988).

The End of the World

A version of this beautiful and mysterious story can be found in Richard Erdoes and Alfonso Ortiz's *American Indian Myths and Legends* (Pantheon Books, New York, 1984), in my opinion the best anthology of First Nation stories.

Riddles

The riddles in this book have been accumulated over many years. Some of them I've heard from the children I've met in the many schools, fairs, libraries and theatres in which I've told stories. Some I've heard from fellow storytellers, most notably Duncan Williamson, Taffy Thomas, Daniel Morden and Helen East. Certain books have also been invaluable: Mark Bryant's *Riddles Ancient and Modern* (Hutchinson, London, 1983); O. J. Halliwell's *Popular Rhymes and Nursery Tales of England* (Bodley Head, London, 1970); A. Jablow's *Yes and No: The Intimate Folklore of Africa* (Horizon Press, New York, 1961); *Mother Goose's Nursery Rhymes and Tales* (Frederick Warne, London, 1890); Iona and Peter Opie's *The Oxford Nursery Rhyme Book* (Oxford University Press, Oxford, 1955); Carl Withers and Sula Benet's *Riddles of Many Lands* (Abelard-Schuman, New York, 1956).

Pages 25-26
'A Great Wonder' and 'A moth devoured words' are from the Exeter Book Riddles (transcribed in the tenth century). Two excellent translations of the riddles in this collection are *A Feast of Creatures* by Craig Williamson (Scolar Press, London, 1983) and *The Exeter Book Riddles* by Kevin Crossley-Holland (Penguin Books, Harmondsworth, 1979).

Pages 38-39
'Gollum's Riddle' is one of the riddles from a riddling contest between Bilbo Baggins and Gollum in chapter five of J. R. R. Tolkien's *The Hobbit* (George Allen & Unwin, London, 1937). Read it for yourself, or better still read the whole book!

The great Greek poet and storyteller is supposed to have died of frustration trying to guess 'The riddle that killed Homer' (put to him by some fishermen on the island of Ios).

In ancient Greek myth, the Sphinx was a monster — part lion, part eagle, part woman. She put this question to all travellers entering the city of Thebes. All those unable to find the answer — and none could — she devoured. Finally a hero called Oedipus answered the riddle and saved the city.

In Lewis Carroll's *Alice's Adventures in Wonderland* the Mad Hatter never answers this riddle. When Lewis Carroll was asked for the answer, he suggested: 'Because it can produce a few notes, though they are *very* flat.' My favourite solution comes from America's great puzzle designer Sam Loyd (in his *Cyclopedia of Puzzles*, 1914): 'Because Poe wrote on both.' (The American author Edgar Allan Poe wrote a poem called 'The Raven'.)

Page 45
Jonathan Swift (1667–1745) is best known for writing *Gulliver's Travels*. He was also a prolific inventor of riddles. The riddle 'Little Airy Creatures' can be found in *Riddles Ancient and Modern* by Mark Bryant (Hutchinson, London, 1983).

Answers to the Riddles

Page 1
A story

Pages 8-9
A candle
An umbrella
The letter M
My son
A stamp

Pages 10-11
Smoke
The stars
An egg
A breath
A violin (the 'horse' refers to the violin bow, which is made of horsehair. The 'cat' refers to the fact that violin strings are traditionally made from catgut)

Pages 16-17
A person is sitting on a stool eating a chicken leg, a dog seizes the chicken leg, so the person throws the stool at the dog and it brings back the chicken leg
A hole
A person on horseback
A tree covered with snow

Pages 18-19
A leg
A football team
A cabbage (the 'leg' refers to its root, and the 'heart' refers to the dense part of the cabbage in the very centre of its 'head')

Page 25 (see also Notes and Sources)
Ice

Pages 26-27 (see also Notes and Sources)
A bookworm
The moon
A person on horseback (hat, rider, saddle, horse, horseshoe, turf)
A pack of cards

Pages 36-37
Shoes
A jersey or sweater
Your name
The number one
A towel
Needles and pins

Pages 38–39 (see also Notes and Sources)
Time
Fleas
A human being
'… I give up,' Alice replied. 'What's the answer?'
'I haven't the slightest idea,' said the Hatter.
'Nor I,' said the March Hare.
Alice sighed wearily. 'I think you might do something better with the time,' she said, 'than wasting it in asking riddles that have no answers.' (For possible solutions to this riddle, see Notes and Sources.)

Page 45 (see also Notes and Sources)
The vowels

Pages 46-47
The eyes
A secret
Silence
A ball of wool
The road you're travelling along
A shoe
A needle and thread

Pages 54-55
A dream
A light-bulb
A box of matches
Ears

Pages 56-57
A raisin
Tears
Buttons

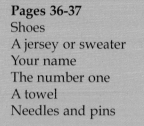